The Village

Vintage Style Coloring Book

Rural Landscapes, Old Rusty Houses to Color – Romantic Antique Sketches

Rachel Mintz

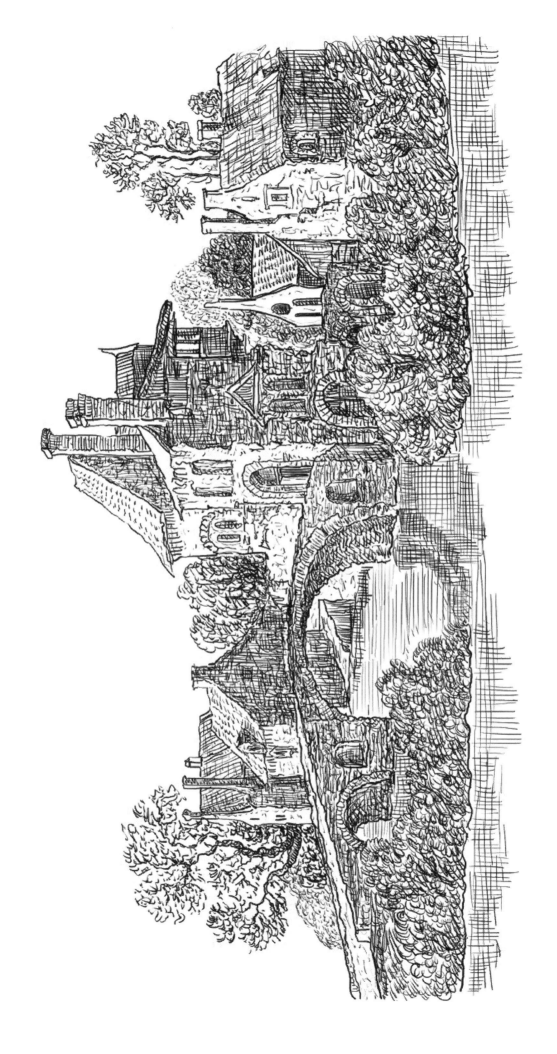

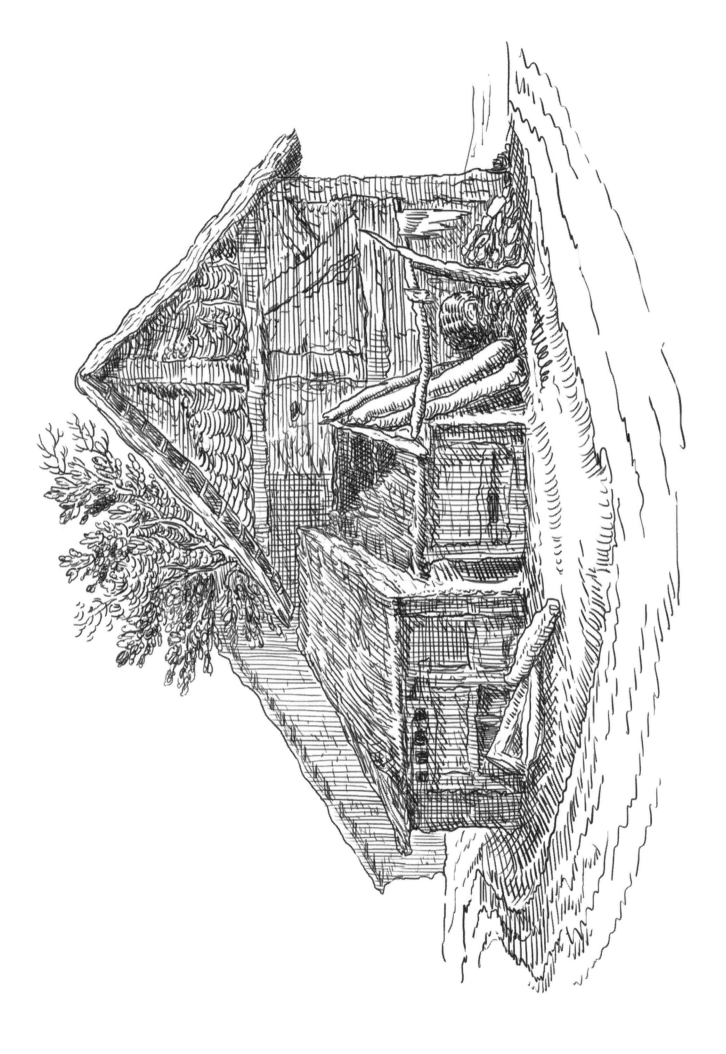

Thank you for coloring with us

More from our coloring books:

Seahorses
Coloring Book

Rachel Mintz

Thank you for coloring with us

Made in the USA
Middletown, DE
02 September 2021

47428305R00062